More Masses with Children

8 6.95

D0113125

SISTER FRANCESCA KELLY

MORE MASSES
WITH CHILDREN

the columba press

the columba press
8 Lower Kilmacud Road, Blackrock, Co. Dublin, Ireland.

First edition 1986
Typography by Liam Miller
Cover by Bill Bolger
Typeset in Dublin by
Printset & Design Ltd
Printed in Ireland by
Mount Salus Press

ISBN 0 948183 13 6 (hardback)
ISBN 0 948183 14 4 (paperback)

The publisher acknowledges the gracious permission of William Collins & Sons for permission to use extracts from *Listen* and *Praise*, both by A.J. McCallen.

Copyright ©, 1986, Sr Francesca Kelly

CONTENTS

1. GOD KNOWS ME

The theme of this Mass is the 'specialness' of each one of us. God has made each one of us so special and so different. And yet he knows every one of us, and he knows everything about every one of us. He knows us even by our very own names.

First Prayer
God our Father, we thank you for the 'specialness' of each one of us. Help us to know, love and thank you always for making us your very special children. We make our prayer through Jesus Christ, your Son, who lives and reigns with you in the unity of the Holy Spirit, one God forever and ever. Amen.

First Reading   Gen 25, 26, 27
Then God said:

Let us make people — and he made men and women and put them in charge of the world.

Then God looked at everything and God said: 'It is all very good!'

This is the Word of the Lord.

Responsorial Psalm   Ps 138:1-11
This is a song of praise to God the Father who loves us too much to leave us all on our own.

RESPONSE: You are always close to us, O Lord.

1. You know me Lord, so very well.
   You know when I get up.
   You know when I go back to sleep.
   You know each thing I do. ℟

2. You know what I am going to say before I even speak!
   You are always close to me.
   You're wonderful, O Lord. ℟

7

3. So if I climbed the highest hill,
   you would be there with me.
   And if I swam beneath the waves,
   you'd still be there with me. ℟

4. Even in the dark at night
   you would be next to me.
   Yes, even then I would not hide,
   you would be there with me. ℟

Second Reading   Col 3:12, 16, 17
St Paul tells us in this reading that God wants to get to know us because he loves us.

Dear friends,
Don't forget that God wants to get to know you, because he loves you. But you must help each other to know how much God loves you by singing his songs.

And remember! When you sing these songs, say 'thank you' to God for he is your Father in heaven.

This is the Word of the Lord.

Gospel Acclamation
Alleluia, alleluia,
I know all my sheep, everyone of them, and they know me.
Alleluia.

Gospel Reading   Jn 10:3-5, 14
God looks after us like a shepherd, and he knows us. Jesus looks after us like a shepherd as well, and he knows each of us — even our names.

One day Jesus said:
Sheep listen to their own shepherd and they will follow him.
He can even call them one by one for he knows their names and he can call them out of the sheepfold through the gate.

When they have all come out, he walks in front of them, and they all follow because they know the sound of his voice.

8

Of course, they would never follow a stranger because they would not know the sound of his voice. They would run away from him if he told them to follow him.

Then Jesus said:
I am a shepherd and I am a *good* shepherd.
I know all my sheep, every one of them, and they know me.

This is the Gospel of the Lord.

Prayers of the Faithful

God our Father, we your children, gathered here around your table, bring to you in prayer our own needs and the needs of people far and near.

1. We pray for our fathers and mothers, and for parents all round the world.
   Bless them and help them to know you.
   Lord hear us. ℞

2. We pray for our brothers and sisters, and for brothers and sisters all round the world.
   Bless them and help them to know you.
   Lord hear us. ℞

3. We pray for young people in our parish, and for young people all round the world.
   Bless them and help them to know you.
   Lord hear us. ℞

4. We pray for old people in our parish, and for the elderly all round the world.
   Bless them and help them to know you.
   Lord hear us. ℞

5. We pray for children with special needs in our parish, and for children with special needs all round the world.
   Bless them and help them to know you.
   Lord hear us. ℞

6. We pray for children who are fearful, lonely and treated badly in our parish and all round the world.
   Bless them and help them to know you.
   Lord hear us. ℟

Preparation of the Gifts
1. We bring a lamp of clay.
   We are like the clay, and God is the potter who moulds the clay.
2. We bring a list of our names.
   Each of us is special, and different, and God knows us by our own names.
3. We bring our love with the bread, the wine and the water.

Second Prayer
God our Father, we bring you our gifts and we bring you the 'specialness' of each one of us here today. Bless us all and help us to know you. We make this prayer through Jesus Christ, your Son, who lives and reigns with you in the unity of the Holy Spirit, one God forever and ever. Amen.

Third Prayer
God our Father, Jesus is with us in this Holy Communion. May he help us to remember our own 'specialness', and may he help us to let you continue to mould us like the potter who moulds the clay. We make this prayer through Jesus Christ, your Son, who lives and reigns with you in the unity of the Holy Spirit, one God forever and ever. Amen.

Final Blessing
Go in peace, to know God and to love him.

2. THE FAMILY

The theme of this Mass is the Family. We thank God for our families. We thank him especially for our father and mother, who show us God's love and care in our family.

First Prayer

God our Father, we thank you for our family. Thank you for fathers, mothers, brothers and sisters. Make us glad to be together and help us to love you more. We ask this through Jesus, your Son, who lives and reigns with you in the unity of the Holy Spirit, one God forever and ever. Amen.

First Reading   Ezk 36:24-8

In this reading we are reminded that we are all God's children and that we all belong to his family.

God says:

I want all my people to come back to me and live at home with me again. Your hearts have become hard as stone but I will make you kind and you will do what I will tell you for I will give you my Holy Spirit. I will pour water over you and wash all the dirt away so that you may be clean all over. You will be my family and I will be your father.

This is the Word of the Lord.

Responsorial Psalm   Ps 99:1-5

This is a poem that says 'Thank You' to God, because we know he is so interested in us, his children.

RESPONSE: We thank you, we praise you for you are good and loving.

1. Let everyone be happy
   Let everyone be glad
   Let everyone be full of joy and sing to the Lord. ℟

2. We know the Lord is God,
   He gives us life and breath,
   for we are his own family
   and we belong to him. ℟

11

Second Reading   Rom 12:8, 10, 11, 13
*This reading is from one of the Letters of St Paul. It tells us that God our
Father wants us to love, like Jesus.*

Dear friends,
God is making things better all the time.

He knows all the people who love him, and he gives them each a
job to do so that they can work with him.

He wants us all to become more like Jesus, his Son, for Jesus is our
eldest brother in the family of God.

This is the Word of the Lord.

Gospel Acclamation
Alleluia, alleluia,
You will all be my brothers and my sisters as well,
if you do what God wants you to do.
Alleluia.

Gospel Reading   Mk 3:20, 21, 31-35
*This reading tells us that if we do what God wants us to do we are his brothers,
his sisters and his mother as well.*

One day Jesus went home and so many people came to see him and
he was so busy that he didn't even have time to eat anything.

When his family heard about this they said he was mad, and they
came along to help him. But there were so many people outside the
house they couldn't even get anywhere near him. So they sent him
a message, saying, 'Your mother and the rest of your family are outside
and they want to see you.'

Inside the house everyone was sitting round Jesus in a circle, and he
looked round at them all and said, 'You will all be my brothers and
sisters and my mother as well, if you do what God wants you to do.'

This is the Gospel of the Lord.

Prayers of the Faithful
We thank you God for all your love and goodness.
We pray for the needs of all parents and their children.

1. Bless all our parents.
   Help them to lead their children to you, by word and example.
   Lord hear us. ℞

2. Bless all of us, your children.
   Help us to grow daily in your love.
   Lord hear us. ℞

3. Bless all the parents in this parish.
   Help them to love and care for their children.
   Lord hear us. ℞

4. Bless all the children in this parish.
   Help them always to love and obey their parents.
   Lord hear us. ℞

5. Bless the families of the whole world.
   Fill them with your love and happiness.
   Lord hear us. ℞

6. We pray for our friends who have died.
   Give them eternal rest in their heavenly home.
   Lord hear us. ℞

Preparation of the Gifts
1. We bring a bible.
   Our family grows together in faith.
2. We bring a rosary beads.
   Our family grows together in love.
3. We bring our love with the bread, the wine and the water.

Second Prayer
God our Father, we bring you our gifts of bread and wine. With them, we bring the love and goodness of our family. Help us all to grow in our love for you and for each other. We make our prayer through Jesus, your Son, who lives and reigns with you in the unity of the Holy Spirit, one God forever and ever. Amen.

13

Third Prayer

God our Father, we have come close to your Son in this Communion. Help us to come close to each other in our family. We make our prayer through Jesus, your Son, who lives and reigns with you in the unity of the Holy Spirit, one God forever and ever. Amen.

Final Blessing

Go in peace, to love and thank God for all his love and goodness. Amen.

3. HANDS

The theme of this Mass is hands.
Our hands are very important — we need them to do everything.
We need them to do things for ourselves — playing, dressing, eating, feeling and writing.
We need them to do things for others — sharing, giving, holding, lifting and helping.
We will think about the best ways to use our hands.

First Prayer

God our Father, we thank you for our hands.
We thank you for what we can do with them.
Help us to use them in kind and helpful ways.
We ask this through Jesus, your Son, who lives and reigns with you in the unity of the Holy Spirit, one God forever and ever. Amen.

First Reading

This is the story of Mother Teresa of Calcutta. It is the story of a very kind and generous woman, who uses her hands to help.

Mother Teresa lives in India, in a big city called Calcutta. When she became a nun she felt called to work in the very poor parts of that city. She went to the slums and taught the poor children.

She loved them and cared for them.

She visited the sick and helped them.

She saw many poor people dying on the streets.

She asked the Mayor of Calcutta for help to set up a home for them.

She wanted those dying people to know and to feel that they were wanted. She wanted them to know that they were loved. She wanted them to know that they were God's children and that he will never forget them and will never leave them.

Mother Teresa still uses her hands to comfort the people of Calcutta. She brings happiness to them, and she brings happiness to people everywhere around the world.

Responsorial Psalm   Ps 15:7-9
This is a prayer of thanks to God, because he keeps us safe in his hands.

RESPONSE: Lord God, we are safe with you.

1. We praise the Lord, for he guides us along the right path. ℟
2. By day and by night he shows us what to do. ℟
3. We shall not fall down if he is there beside us. ℟
4. Lord we are happy for we are safe with you. ℟

Second Reading   Is 58:7-8
Isaiah is telling us that we must take care of each other.

You must share things. You must feed the hungry, and get houses for the poor people.
And you must buy clothes for the people who haven't got enough.

If you do this, you will make the whole world bright. You will be like the sun that fills the sky with light each morning.

This is the Word of the Lord.

Gospel Acclamation
Alleluia, alleluia,
Don't stop the children from coming to me.
Bring them back.
Alleluia.

Gospel Reading   Mk 10: 13, 14, 16
Jesus used his hands to do good, to heal and to help.
In this story, he uses his hands to welcome the children, and to bless them.

People often used to bring children to Jesus, and when they did, Jesus always gave them his blessing.

One day, however, some of the friends of Jesus told the children to go away. Jesus was angry when he saw this happening, and he said:

Don't stop the children from coming to me. Don't send them away like that! Bring them back.

Then he put his arms round the children and he blessed them.

This is the Gospel of the Lord.

Prayers of the Faithful

God our Father, we thank you for people who work for us, and we pray for all those who use their hands to help us.

1. Bless our Pope, our bishop and our priests, who bring us your love, and forgiveness.
   Lord hear us. ℟

2. Bless our mammies and daddies, who make our homes warm and loving.
   Lord hear us. ℟

3. Bless our teachers, who make our schools friendly and happy.
   Lord hear us. ℟

4. Bless the doctors and the nurses, who help us in sickness.
   Lord hear us. ℟

5. Bless the farmers and the bakers, who work for our food.
   Lord hear us. ℟

6. Bless our friends, who are always loving and kind.
   Lord hear us. ℟

Preparation of the Gifts

1. We bring our best writing.
2. We bring our best painting.
3. We bring our best handwork.
4. We bring our love with the bread, the wine and the water.

Second Prayer

God our Father, we bring you our hands, and all the work we do with them. Take them with our gifts of bread and wine. We make this prayer through Jesus, your Son, who lives and reigns with you in the unity of the Holy Spirit, one God forever and ever. Amen.

Communion Litany

RESPONSE: We thank you, Lord our God.

1. For kind hands that help at home
   And for kind hands that help at school. ℟

17

RESPONSE: We thank you, Lord our God.

2. For kind hands that bless and pray
   And for kind hands that play happy games. ℟

3. For kind hands that share
   And for kind hands that give gifts. ℟

4. For kind hands that comfort
   And for kind hands that stroke gently. ℟

5. For kind hands that make beautiful things
   And for kind hands that enjoy things. ℟

Third Prayer
God our Father, Jesus is with us now. He used his hands to comfort, to console, to bless and to help. May we use our hands like Jesus. We ask this through Jesus Christ, your Son, who lives and reigns with you in the unity of the Holy Spirit, one God forever and ever. Amen.

Blessing of Hands
A simple ceremony of blessing of hands may take place before the final blessing.
Go in peace, to know God and to love him.

Final Blessing

4. SPEAKING

Today we are thinking about speaking and about the ways God wants us to use this wonderful gift to make people happy.

First Prayer
God our Father, thank you for the gift of speaking. Help us to use our voices to bring happiness to others. We ask this through Jesus, your Son, who lives and reigns with you in the unity of the Holy Spirit, one God forever and ever. Amen.

First Reading   Lev 19:16-18
This reading comes from the Book of Moses. It tells us how God wants us to use our voices.

God says:
You must not tell lies about other people.
You must not hate anyone.

If someone has done wrong,
tell them that they have done wrong
but don't try to get your own back.

Don't grumble either.

You must take care of each other
just as much as you take care of yourself.

This is the Word of the Lord.

Responsorial Psalm   Ps 27:6-7
The responsorial psalm is taken from the Book of Praise. We tell God we know we can always trust him.

RESPONSE: Blessed be God.

1. He listens to me.
   He hears me when I pray for help. ℟

2. I trust the Lord for he is strong. ℟

3. I thank the Lord for he takes care of me. ℟

Second Reading   Jas 3:5, 6, 9

This reading is from some of the letters of St James. He gives us good advice about using the gift of speaking.

The tongue is like a little flame, friendly and warm. But just as a little flame can start a forest fire, the tongue can do very great harm by telling lies and saying unkind things.

My friends:
the tongue speaks your voice. It is holy. It is from God. Always use it to give praise to God.

This is the Word of the Lord.

Gospel Acclamation
Alleluia, alleluia,
I want to sing and to shout because I am so happy.
Alleluia.

Gospel Reading   Lk 17:11-16

This reading is from the gospel of St Luke. It is the story of the man who said "thank you" to Jesus. It shows us that we must never forget to say "thank you".

One day Jesus went up to Jerusalem and while he was on his way he went into a little town nearby.

Ten lepers came out to meet him there, and they waved across to him, saying, "Please help us, Jesus!"

When he saw them, Jesus said, "Go and see the priest!" So they did, and as they were on their way, they were healed!

One of the ten came straight back to Jesus and he praised God at the top of his voice, throwing himself down in front of Jesus. "Thank you, Jesus", he said, "Thank you very much!"

This is the Gospel of the Lord.

Prayers of the Faithful
God our Father, we thank you for all your gifts, especially the gift of speaking. We pray for all those who use this gift to make you better known and loved.

1. We pray for our Holy Father, Pope John Paul, who often speaks to us about God's love.
   Lord hear us. ℞

2. We pray for our mothers and fathers who tell us about God's love.
   Lord hear us. ℞

3. We pray for our priests and teachers who pass on God's message of love in school.
   Lord hear us. ℞

4. We pray for missionaries who spread God's message of love in faraway countries.
   Lord hear us. ℞

5. We pray for all those who speak out bravely for justice and peace.
   Lord hear us. ℞

6. We thank you for the gift of speaking. We pray for people with speaking difficulties.
   Lord hear us. ℞

Preparation of the Gifts
1. We bring a bible for God's spoken word.
2. We bring a newspaper for everyday news.
3. We bring a radio for news, views and music.
4. We bring our love with the bread, the wine and the water.

Second Prayer
God our Father, we give you ourselves with these gifts of bread and wine. Help us always to use our voices well — to praise you, to offer help, to give comfort and to say "thanks". We make our prayer through Jesus, your Son, who lives and reigns with you in the unity of the Holy Spirit, one God forever and ever. Amen.

Third Prayer
God our Father, your Son Jesus is with us now. May he stay with us always and help us to bring peace and joy to everybody. We make this prayer through Jesus, your Son, who lives and reigns with you in the unity of the Holy Spirit, one God forever and ever. Amen.

Final Blessing
Go in peace, to love God and to praise him with your voice.

5. TREES

The theme of this Mass is trees. God has made the world beautiful with trees — trees of every shape and every size. Trees remind us of God's power, love and care. Today we praise God for his love and care.

First Prayer

God our Father, trees show your power and love, at work in the world. Help us to remember your love and care, when we see trees all around us. We ask this through Jesus, your Son, who lives and reigns with you in the unity of the Holy Spirit, one God forever and ever. Amen.

First Reading   Ps 1:3

Each year God cares for the trees. God cares for us too, looks after us, and protects us.

Down by the river is a good place for trees.

If the water flows near them, they never grow dry.
Their leaves are not withered, they stay green and alive.
And each year their branches are covered with fruit.

The man that is good is like a tree by the river.

God will look after him;
God will protect him
and like a tree by the river he will grow strong.

This is the Word of the Lord.

Responsorial Psalm   Ps 49:10-11

Everything belongs to God. We praise him.

RESPONSE: Blessed be God.

1. Whenever you see the animals in the woods, they belong to me. ℟

2. Whenever you see the cattle on the hillsides, remember who made them. ℟

3. Whenever you see the birds up on the treetops, remember, I know each one of them. ℟

4. Whenever you see a living thing out in the fields, think of me. ℟

Second Reading
Song 2:11-13

Trees change all the time. In springtime each year they grow new leaves. God looks after the trees at all times.

Whenever Winter is finished, and the rain has stopped falling, then the plants begin to grow.

The birds sing and leaves appear on the trees and at last you can smell the perfume of the flowers.

This is the time to sing for joy.

This is the Word of the Lord.

Gospel Acclamation
Alleluia, alleluia,
God said:
Let plants grow in the soil and let there be fruit trees.
Alleluia.

Gospel Reading
Mk 4:30-33

St Mark tells us that God cares for the animals too, and gives them the trees for their homes.

One day Jesus said:
The mustard seed is the smallest seed in the world, but when you plant it in the ground it grows and becomes so big that the birds can come and build their nests in the shade of its branches.

Then Jesus said:
God works like that.

This is the Gospel of the Lord.

Prayers of the Faithful
God our Father, we thank you for loving and caring for our families and our friends. We pray today for all those who help to make us happy.

1. We pray for those who cut wood in the forests and work in the timber mills. Show them your love and care.
   Lord hear us. ℟

2. We pray for the builders, who use wood in our homes. Show them your love and care.
Lord hear us. ℟

3. We pray for carpenters, who make furniture for our homes. Show them your love and care.
Lord hear us. ℟

4. We pray for furnishers, who make seats for our churches, and desks for our schools. Show them your love and care.
Lord hear us. ℟

5. We pray for wood carvers, who carve wooden statues and other beautiful things. Show them your love and care.
Lord hear us. ℟

Preparation of the Gifts
1. We bring a chair.
2. We bring a guitar.
3. We bring a carved statue.
4. We bring our love with the bread, the wine and the water.

Second Prayer
God our Father, we bring you ourselves with our gifts of bread and wine. Through your power, love and care, make our gifts and our lives into something great. We ask this through Jesus, your Son, who lives and reigns with you in the unity of the Holy Spirit, one God forever and ever. Amen.

Communion Litany
RESPONSE: Praise the Lord for trees.

1. For trees, with pale fresh green leaves in Spring.
And for trees, with yellow, red, brown and gold leaves in Autumn. ℟

2. For trees, bare and leafless in Winter,
And for living trees, hidden in coats of bark. ℟

3. For trees with long, twisting branches,
And for trees that reach high in the sky. ℟

4. For trees that are homes for birds and insects
   And for trees that shelter animals from rain. ℞

5. For trees that make wood for building homes
   And for trees that make furniture for our homes. ℞

Third Prayer

God our Father, Jesus your Son is close to us now. Help us to stay close to him, and to grow up to you like a tree — tall and strong. We ask this through Jesus, your Son, who lives and reigns with you in the unity of the Holy Spirit, one God forever and ever. Amen.

Final Blessing

Go in peace, to love God.

6. THE MISSIONS

Today we pray for the Missions.
We think especially of people who leave their families, their homes, and their country to bring the Good News of God's love, to people and children around the world who do not know about God.

First Prayer
God our Father, you love all children. Help us to love you, and to help our brothers and sisters around the world to know and love you. We make our prayer through Jesus, your Son, who lives and reigns with you in the unity of the Holy Spirit, one God forever and ever. Amen.

First Reading   Is 60:2a, 1, 2b
Isaiah, the Wise Man, tells us that the sun rises in the sky every day and fills the world with light.
Jesus is like that as well, — only he fills the world with happiness and goodness.

In the beginning,
the world was filled with darkness and it was as black as night.
But God came and changed all that!
He filled the world with his light instead,
just like the sun that shines in the sky every morning.

This is the Word of the Lord.

Responsorial Psalm   Ps 27:6, 7
This is a song of praise and trust in God.
RESPONSE: Blessed be God.

1. He listens to me,
   he hears me when I pray for help. ℞

2. I trust the Lord
   for he is strong. ℞

3. I thank the Lord
   for he takes care of me. ℞

26

Second Reading   1 Jn 3: 1, 4, 7-8
St John tells us that God is our Father and that we are his children. He takes care of us and loves us all.

Dear friends,
See how much God thinks of us. He calls us his children, and we really are, you know.

God takes care of us, so we must take care of each other.

God loves us, so we must love each other.

If we don't know that, we don't know anything about God our Father, because 'God *is* Love'.

This is the Word of the Lord.

Gospel Acclamation
Alleluia, alleluia.
Go out to the whole world, tell everyone what I have done.
Alleluia.

Gospel Reading   Mk 16:15-16, 20
In this reading Jesus is telling his friends to spread the Good News, everywhere in the whole world.

One day, Jesus said to his friends:
'Go out to the whole world. Tell everyone what I have done and baptise everyone who believes what you say.'

And they did just that: after Jesus had died, they talked about him everywhere.
And even though they could not see him, Jesus helped them all the time.

This is the Gospel of the Lord.

Prayers of the Faithful
God our Father, you sent Jesus, the first missionary, on his great mission. We pray for the friends of Jesus in faraway countries today. Help them to spread the love of Jesus around the world, and to help everyone to be friends.

1. We pray for priests who work around the world.
   Be with them as they work.
   Lord hear us. ℟

2. We pray for sisters who work around the world.
   Be with them as they work.
   Lord hear us. ℟

3. We pray for lay people who work around the world.
   Be with them as they work.
   Lord hear us. ℟

4. We pray for people around the world, who do not know about Jesus.
   Be with them as they work.
   Lord hear us. ℟

5. We pray for children around the world, who do not know about Jesus.
   Be with them as they work.
   Lord hear us. ℟

Preparation of the Gifts
1. We bring a lighted candle.
   We help people and children to be friends of Jesus.
2. We bring a globe.
   We help everyone in the world to be friends together.
3. We bring our mission boxes.
   We help especially by sharing what we have.

Second Prayer
God our Father, we bring you our gifts of bread and wine. With them we bring ourselves, and our brothers and sisters around the world. Take us all in the name of Jesus Christ, your Son, who lives and reigns with you in the unity of the Holy Spirit, one God forever and ever. Amen.

Third Prayer
God our Father, may this Holy Communion help us to love each other and to love our brothers and sisters around the world. We make our prayer through Jesus Christ, your Son, who lives and reigns with you in the unity of the Holy Spirit, one God forever and ever. Amen.

Final Blessing
Go in peace, to love God, and to help and share with your brothers and sisters around the world.

7. BEING GREAT FOR GOD

Today we are thinking about being great for God. We know some people who are great — they try to do something really well. The saints were all great people. They were great for God. We can be like them.

First Prayer

God our Father, you are great. You sent us Jesus who was great. Help us to be great — to be your friends and followers. We ask this through Jesus, your Son, who lives and reigns with you in the unity of the Holy Spirit, one God forever and ever. Amen.

First Reading

This reading is part of a poem which thanks God for his greatness in giving us beautiful things.

We thank you, Lord of heaven,
For the joys that greet us,
For all that you have given
To help and delight us
In earth and sky and seas;
The sunlight on the meadows,
The rainbow's fleeting wonder,
The clouds with cooling shadows,
The stars that shine in splendour —
We thank you, Lord, for these.

Jan Struther

Responsorial Psalm   Ps 17:8-9, 12-16

RESPONSE: Lord God, you are great and powerful.

1. God is as strong as an earthquake that shakes the whole world and makes the mountains tremble! ℞

2. God is as strong as a volcano that splits the land open, pouring out fire and burning flames and clouds of smoke. ℞

3. God is as powerful as a thunderstorm at night when everything is dark, and lightning flashes across the sky, cutting through the heavy rain clouds like an arrow! ℞

4. God is as powerful as the mighty sound of thunder rumbling overhead like a deep and angry roar. ℞

Second Reading   Rom 15:17-19
This reading is about St Paul. He wrote this about himself:

I'm proud of what I've been able to do to make God's way known throughout the world. But only through Jesus I have been able to do what I have done.

There is one thing — and one thing only — I care to talk about: how Jesus has used me to help people of many lands to live in God's way. From Jerusalem to Palestine, all round the world I have made the good news of Jesus sound like the good news it is — good news for everybody. For I have had one ambition: to tell the story of Jesus where his name had never been heard.

This is the Word of the Lord.

Third Reading   1 Cor 9:5; Gal 1:19;
Rom 1:4 and 15:3; 1 Thess 1:6;
Gal 5:22-23; Phil 4:23
This reading comes from St Paul's letters. It tells us how great Jesus was.

He cared for people — for everybody. He was a very happy man. People who couldn't get on with one another found it possible to be friends in his presence. He never gave up. He was very kind, a really good man, and he could always be relied upon. He was gentle, yet master of himself.
What people remembered about him was his graciousness.

This is the Word of the Lord.

Gospel Acclamation
Alleluia, alleluia,
Believe me, when you helped the least of my brothers, you helped me.
Alleluia.

31

Gospel Reading   Mt 25:35-37, 40

The Gospel reading is from the gospel of St Matthew. Jesus often told his friends that they would be truly great if they served others. They would prove they were his friends if he could say to them:

"I was hungry and you gave me food;
I was thirsty and you gave me drink;
I was a foreigner and you took me home with you;
I was in rags and you gave me clothes;
I fell ill and you looked after me;
I was in prison and you came to see me.
Believe me –
when you helped the least of my brothers,
you helped me."

This is the Gospel of the Lord.

Prayers of the Faithful

1. Mary was obedient and did what God asked her to do.
   Help us to be great and to do what we are told.
   Lord hear us. ℞

2. St Veronica was kind to Jesus on the way to Calvary.
   Help us to be great and to be kind and loving.
   Lord hear us. ℞

3. St Bernadette loved Mary and prayed to her often.
   Help us to be great and to love Mary, our Mother.
   Lord hear us. ℞

4. St Stephen was quick to forgive his enemies.
   Help us to be great and to forgive like him.
   Lord hear us. ℞

5. St. Vincent cared for the sick and the poor.
   Help us to be great, to comfort the sick and help the poor.
   Lord hear us. ℞

6. St. Patrick spent long hours praying.
   Help us to be great and to pray often.
   Lord hear us. ℞

Preparation of the Gifts
We bring gifts to show that like all great artists, we must not give up trying to be great.
1. We bring a football.
2. We bring a musical instrument.
3. We bring a pair of dancing shoes.
4. We bring our love with the bread, the wine and the water.

Second Prayer
God our Father, we bring you ourselves with all our gifts. Help us to bring joy, love and peace to all our friends. We ask this through Jesus, your Son, who lives and reigns with you in the unity of the Holy Spirit, one God forever and ever. Amen.

Third Prayer
God our Father, you have given us your Son. Jesus is great. May he help us to be great too. We ask this through Jesus, your Son, who lives and reigns with you in the unity of the Holy Spirit, one God forever and ever. Amen.

Final Blessing
Go in peace, to know God and to love him.

8. CHRIST THE KING

The theme of this Mass is Christ the King.
Christ is our King, and he is King of the world. We live in his Kingdom and we are his loyal children. Today, we renew our love and our loyalty to Christ the King.

First Prayer

God our Father, you have given us your Son, to be our Lord and King. Help us to be loyal followers in his Kingdom. We ask this through Jesus, your Son, who lives and reigns with you in the unity of the Holy Spirit, one God forever and ever. Amen.

First Reading   Is 9:1-2, 6-7

This reading is from the Book of a wise man called Isaiah. He is saying that God the Father would send us Jesus to be our King.

Once upon a time,
everyone lived in the dark
but now we can see!

They used to live in a world
that was full of shadows
but now we have a light,
to light up our way!
We have God with us
and he has made us happy.

He has sent us a child
who is to be our King,
and he will keep everyone safe.

This is the Word of the Lord.

Responsorial Psalm   Ps 46:2-3, 6, 8

This is a poem from the Book of Praise.
We praise the greatness of the King of all the earth.

RESPONSE: The Lord is King of the whole wide world.

1. Clap your hands and shout for joy. ℟

2. Play the trumpet loud and clear. ℞

3. Sing and praise him, everyone! ℞

4. Praise him now with all your skills. ℞

Second Reading
Eph 1: 20, 21, 22

St Paul tells us that God the Father has made Jesus the King of the World.

Dear friends,
Jesus died — he was killed! But God the Father has raised him to life again. He has made Jesus the King of the World, and put him in charge of everything.

In fact God the Father has made him greater than anybody else.

This is the Word of the Lord.

Gospel Acclamation
Alleluia, alleluia,
Peter said:
You are the Great King that God promised to send us.
Alleluia.

Gospel Reading
Mk 8: 27-30

When Jesus asked his friends who they thought he was, Peter said that Jesus was the great king that God had promised.

One day Jesus and his friends were walking along the road and he suddenly said,
'Who do people think I am?'

His friends said, 'Some people think you are John the Baptist! And other people think you are one of the great teachers!'

Then Jesus said, 'Who do you think I am?'
And Peter said, 'You are the Great King that God promised to send us.'

This is the Gospel of the Lord.

Prayers of the Faithful
God our Father, we your children, gathered round your table, call to you in prayer. We ask you in faith and love to hear us.

1. We pray for our Pope, our bishops, and our priests.
   May your kingdom come in their hearts.
   Lord hear us. ℞

2. We pray for our families and for our friends.
   May your kingdom come in their hearts.
   Lord hear us. ℞

3. We pray for people who are sad and lonely.
   May your kingdom come in their hearts.
   Lord hear us. ℞

4. We pray for people who are sick and weak.
   May your kingdom come in their hearts.
   Lord hear us. ℞

5. We pray for our teachers, and for those who work for us in school.
   May your kingdom come in their hearts.
   Lord hear us. ℞

Preparation of the Gifts
1. We bring a crown.
   Jesus is our King.
2. We bring our love with the bread, the wine and the water.

Second Prayer
God our Father, we bring you our gifts of bread and wine. We bring with them our love and loyalty to Christ our King. We make our prayer through Jesus, your Son, who lives and reigns with you in the unity of the Holy Spirit, one God forever and ever. Amen.

Third Prayer
God our Father, Christ our King has come to us. May we take him with us, and live happily in his kingdom here on earth. We make our prayer through Jesus, your Son, who lives and reigns with you in the unity of the Holy Spirit, one God forever and ever. Amen.

Final Blessing
Go in peace, to love God.

9. ADVENT

In this Advent theme we think about our response to God's call to love. We say sorry to God for the times we say 'no'. During Advent we make an effort to say 'yes' to God and to follow his way of love.

First Prayer

God our Father, help us during this time of Advent to be your friends. Help us to see the wrong in our lives and make us ready to follow your way of love. We make this prayer through Jesus, your Son, who lives and reigns with you in the unity of the Holy Spirit, one God forever and ever. Amen.

First Reading   Is: 1-2, 6-7

Isaiah tells us that Jesus is like a bright light. His light lights up the path we must walk on our way to God the Father.

Once upon a time, everyone lived in the dark
but now — we can see!
They used to live in a world that was full of shadows
but now — we have a light to light up our way!
We have God with us and he has made us happy.
He has sent us a child who is to be our King, and he will keep everyone safe.

This is the Word of the Lord.

Responsorial Psalm   Ps 10

If we stay close to God our Father, we will be safe and secure.

RESPONSE: God our Father, we will stay close to you.

1. I won't fly away when people attack me.
   I trust in the Lord and I will be safe. ℟

2. I know he can see me — he can see everybody.
   He knows who is good and he knows who is bad. ℟

3. Because he is so good, he loves to see goodness.
   He hates to see violence. ℟

4. So we can be sure if we do what is right
   we can live close beside him safe and secure. ℟

37

Second Reading Eph 1:3-6
*St Paul tells us that God our Father loves us. He loves us in the same way
as he loves his Son, Jesus, because we also are his children!
That's why we say 'thank you' to him.*

Dear friends,
Give thanks to God the Father.
He has made us brothers of Christ!

Even before the world was made,
he chose us to be his very own people
— the People of Christ.

He wanted us to live like him
— in goodness and friendship,
for he had decided that we should be his own children.

He loved us so much that he wanted us to be his sons and daughters.

Let us praise God.

This is the Word of the Lord.

Gospel Acclamation
Alleluia, alleluia,
Someone is coming after me
and he is much more important than I am.
Alleluia.

Gospel Reading Lk 3: 10-11, 14-16
*In this reading St Luke tells us that John the Baptist prepared the way for
Jesus. He told the people what they should do to change their lives and to
follow the way of the Lord.*

Lots of people came to John the Baptist and said:
'What have we got to do?'

John said: 'Share things with each other, and don't be greedy either!'

Everyone thought John was going to be the Great King, and they
all began to get excited.

But John said: 'I am not the Great King that God promised to send.
Someone else is coming after me, and he is much more important

than I am. 'In fact, he is so great that I am not even good enough to untie his shoe-laces!'

This is the Gospel of the Lord.

Prayers of the Faithful
God our Father, we come to you today with all our needs and the needs of all our friends.

1. Bless our Holy Father, the Pope, our bishops, and our priests.
   Help them to follow your way.
   Lord hear us. ℟

2. Bless all our friends.
   Help them to follow your way.
   Lord hear us. ℟

3. Bless our teachers and all who work for us.
   Help them to follow your way.
   Lord hear us. ℟

4. Bless all of us your children.
   Help us to follow your way.
   Lord hear us. ℟

5. Bless all our friends at home and away.
   Help them to follow your way.
   Lord hear us. ℟

Preparation of the Gifts
1. We bring a lighted candle (or Advent wreath).
   Jesus is the light that lights up our way.
2. We bring a bible.
   Jesus is the way to the Father.
3. We bring our love with the bread, the wine and the water.

Second Prayer
God our Father, we bring you our gifts of bread and wine and we bring ourselves with our gifts. Bless our gifts and bless us too. We make our prayer through Jesus, your Son, who lives and reigns with you in the unity of the Holy Spirit, one God forever and ever. Amen.

Third Prayer
God our Father, you have given us your Son Jesus. Help us to stay close to him always and to follow his way of love. We make this prayer through Jesus, your Son, who lives and reigns with you in the unity of the Holy Spirit, one God forever and ever. Amen.

Final Blessing
Go in peace, to love God.

10. LIGHT

This theme is about light, and light is very important to us. In the bright summer days we get a lot of light. In the dark winter days we get less light. Light reminds us of Jesus, who was sent to be our light. He is very important to us too, because he is our very special light. He shows us the way to the Father.

First Prayer

God our Father, we thank you for the brightness of light. Thank you, too, for sending us Jesus to be our light. Help us to follow him always. We make our prayer through Jesus, your Son, who lives and reigns with you in the unity of the Holy Spirit, one God forever and ever. Amen.

First Reading   Gen 1: 1-3

God knows the importance of light, and how terrible it would be if there was none. So he gave us light.

In the beginning the world was all empty, and everything was dark and gloomy. But God was there like the wind that blows over the sea. And God said: 'Let there be light!' And there was light!

And the light was wonderful.

This is the Word of the Lord.

Responsorial Psalm   Ps 17:2, 4, 29

It is wonderful to be able to see, and we thank God for it. This is a prayer of thanks.

RESPONSE: Lord, you are my light.

1. I love you, my Lord,
   for you have made me strong. ℞

2. I thank you, my Lord,
   for you have heard my prayer. ℞

3. You have been like a light before my eyes. ℞

4. You have made my darkness into light. ℞

Second Reading   1 Jn 1: 5-7
St John tells us that when we do good we walk in God's light, and we stay close to him.

Dear friends,
God is light!
If we do wrong, we turn away from the light of God
and go off into the dark.

Some people think they can be close to God and still do wrong.
But they are making a mistake!

The light of God shines on us to help us to do things right and be happy with everyone.

This is the Word of the Lord.

Gospel Acclamation   Jn 7:12
Alleluia, alleluia,
I am the Light of the World,
says the Lord.
Anyone who follows me will have the light of life.
Alleluia.

Gospel Reading   Lk 2:23-32
Simeon and Anna thanked God for letting them see Jesus, 'The Light of the World.'

When Jesus was born Joseph and Mary took him to the Temple in Jerusalem, and offered him to God as the Bible told them to do.

When they came to the Temple, they met an old man called Simeon. Simeon was a good man and the Holy Spirit was very close to him. And as soon as he saw Jesus he took him in his arms, and said:

'Thank you, God our Father. Now I am happy to die, for I have seen Jesus, the Light of the World!'

This is the Gospel of the Lord.

Prayers of the Faithful
God our Father, we know you are with us, and that you listen to us. We bring our needs before you now, in prayer.

1. We pray for our Pope, our bishops and our priests.
   Be a light to them, and help them as they lead us to you.
   Lord hear us. ℟

2. We pray for our country.
   Be a light to our leaders, and bless their work for peace and happiness.
   Lord hear us. ℟

3. We pray for our families.
   Be a light to us in our homes, and help us to follow your way of love.
   Lord hear us. ℟

4. We pray for the children at school.
   Be a light to us, and help us to live as children of light.
   Lord hear us. ℟

5. We pray for missionaries.
   Be a light to them, and help them to bring your light to people in faraway places.
   Lord hear us. ℟

Preparation of the Gifts
1. We bring a candle.
   Jesus is our Light.
2. We bring a torch and a light bulb.
   We will walk in the light.
3. We bring our love with the bread, the wine and the water.

Second Prayer
God our Father, take our gifts of bread and wine. Take our lives too, and help us to live in the light of Jesus. We ask this through Jesus, your Son, who lives and reigns with you in the unity of the Holy Spirit, one God forever and ever. Amen.

Communion Litany
RESPONSE: We thank you, Lord our God.

1. For Jesus, the Light of the World. ℟
2. For the sunlight, that brightens our days. ℟

RESPONSE: We thank you, Lord our God.

3. For the moon and stars that shine in the night. ℞
4. For the lightning, that shows your splendour and power. ℞
5. For the rainbow, that colours the sky. ℞

Third Prayer
God our Father, you have given us Jesus, our Light. May we follow his way of life, and find true peace and happiness in our lives. We make this prayer through Jesus, your Son, who lives and reigns with you in the unity of the Holy Spirit, one God forever and ever. Amen.

Final Blessing
Go in peace, to love God.

11. MARY, MOTHER OF JESUS

The theme is Mary, Mother of Jesus.
Mary prepared for the coming of Jesus in a very special way. When God chose her to be the mother of Jesus, she said 'Yes' to God, that she would be the mother of Jesus. Mary always said 'Yes' to God.

First Prayer
God our Father, we have come together to thank you for Mary, Mother of Jesus, and our mother too. She always did what you wanted her to do. Help us to listen to you, and to do what you want with joy. We make our prayer through Jesus, your Son, who lives and reigns with you in the unity of the Holy Spirit, one God forever and ever. Amen.

First Reading   Is 41:9-10
Isaiah tells us that God chooses every one of us to do a special job in life. But whatever he wants us to do he promises to help us to do it well.

God says:
'I have chosen you.
You are working for me now.
So do not be afraid.
I am with you — don't worry!
I am your God, and I will make you strong.
You can hold my hand and I will help you.'

This is the Word of the Lord.

Responsorial Psalm   Lk 1:46-55
This is Mary's song of love, praise and thanks to God. She was full of joy and happiness.

RESPONSE: God has been good to me.

1. Mary said, "My heart sings with thanks.
   God is great and good.
   Holy is his name. ℞

2. "God has smiled on me.
God looks kindly on all poor people.
Holy is his name. ℟

3. "God is mighty and powerful.
He has done great things for me.
Holy is his name. ℟

4. "God remembers his people.
He has done marvelous deeds for me.
Holy is his name." ℟

Second Reading   Is 12:4-6
God our Father is wonderful.
With Mary, we would like to tell the whole wide world how good he is!

I want to tell the whole wide world
— God has been good to me.

I want to tell the whole wide world
— God is wonderful.

I want to sing and to shout, because I am happy.
For God has come to me, and he is great.

This is the Word of the Lord.

Gospel Acclamation
Alleluia, alleluia,
Rejoice, Mary,
for the Lord has blessed you,
and he is with you, now!
Alleluia.

Gospel Reading   Lk 1:26-31, 38
When God chose Mary to be the Mother of Jesus she said 'Yes — I'll do
anything you want!'

One day
God sent his messenger
to a town called Nazareth
to a girl called Mary
who was engaged to a man called Joseph.

The Messenger said,
'Rejoice, Mary,
for the Lord has blessed you,
and he is with you now!'

Mary didn't know what to say
and she wondered what this meant.
But the messenger said:
'Do not be afraid —
God is very pleased with you.

'Listen
You are going to have a baby,
and you will call him Jesus.'

Then Mary said:
'I am the servant of God.
I am glad to do whatever he wants.'

This is the Gospel of the Lord.

Prayers of the Faithful
God our Father, we ask you now to bless us and to help us always
to do what you want us to do.

1. We pray for our Pope, our bishop and our priests.
   Help them to do what God wants them to do.
   Lord hear us. ℟

2. We pray for our parents, our brothers and our sisters.
   Help them to do what God wants them to do.
   Lord hear us. ℟

3. We pray for our teachers, and all our friends at school.
   Help them to do what God wants them to do.
   Lord hear us. ℟

4. We pray for the people who work for us.
   Help them to do what God wants them to do.
   Lord hear us. ℟

5. We pray for ourselves, and for children everywhere.
   Help them to do what God wants them to do.
   Lord hear us. ℟

Preparation of the Gifts

1. We bring a statue of Mary.
   Mary did what God wanted her to do.
2. We bring a bible.
   Mary listened to God and said 'Yes' to him.
3. We bring a rose.
   We show our love for Mary.
4. We bring our love with the bread, the wine and the water.

Second Prayer

God our Father, we bring our gifts and ourselves to you. Take us and bless us and help us to do always what you want us to do. We make our prayer through Jesus, your Son, who lives and reigns with you in the unity of the Holy Spirit, one God forever and ever. Amen.

Communion Litany

RESPONSE: Thank you God, for Mary.

1. Mary was the Mother of Jesus, at Bethlehem. ℟
2. Mary loved and cared for Jesus. ℟
3. Mary brought Jesus to the Temple for the Presentation. ℟
4. Mary brought Jesus on pilgrimage to Jerusalem. ℟
5. Mary saw Jesus leave home to tell the Good News. ℟
6. Mary was with Jesus as he died on the cross. ℟
7. Mary saw Jesus when he rose from the dead. ℟
8. Mary was with the apostles when the Holy Spirit came to them. ℟

Third Prayer

God our Father, Jesus has come to us in this Holy Communion. Help us to stay close to him as we try to do what God wants us to do. We make this prayer through Jesus, your Son, who lives and reigns with you in the unity of the Holy Spirit, one God forever and ever. Amen.

Final Blessing

Go in peace, to do what God wants you to do. Amen.

12. CHRISTMAS

Today is Christmas Day — a day of joy.
The birth of Jesus brought joy to the world.
It brought joy to Mary and Joseph, the shepherds and the wise men.
Today we share the joy of Mary and Joseph, the shepherds and the wise men.

First Prayer

God our Father, you sent your Son Jesus to show us your love, and to help us to love. Help us to listen to him and to do what you want us to do. We make our prayer through Jesus, your Son, who lives and reigns with you in the unity of the Holy Spirit, one God forever and ever. Amen.

First Reading   Is 60: 1, 26, 29

Isaiah tells us in this reading that Jesus is like the sun that fills the world with daylight. He filled the world with happiness, goodness and joy.

In the beginning, the world was filled with darkness, and it was as black as night.

But God came and changed all that!
He filled the world with his light instead, just like the sun that shines in the sky every morning.

This is the Word of the Lord.

Responsorial Psalm   Ps 17: 2, 4, 29

This is a song of praise, joy and thanks to God because he has been so good to us.

RESPONSE: God has been good to us.

1. I love you, my Lord,
   for you have made me strong. ℞

2. I thank you, my Lord,
   for you have heard my prayer. ℞

3. You have been like a light before my eyes.
   You have made my darkness into light. ℞

4. I thank you, my Lord,
   for you have heard my prayer. ℞

Second Reading Gal 4:4-6
St Paul tells us that Jesus came to help us all. He came to give us the chance to be God's children and part of God's family.

Dear friends,
When the right time came,
God the Father sent Jesus to us.

Jesus had a mother just like the rest of us and he had to do as he was told — like us.

He wanted to help us all, and he came to give us the chance to become like 'Children of God,' so that we called call God 'Our Father' — like him.

This is the Word of the Lord.

Gospel Acclamation
Alleluia, alleluia,
Glory to God in the highest
and peace to his people on earth.
Alleluia.

Gospel Reading Lk 2:4-7
This is the story of the birth of Jesus in Bethlehem.

Joseph lived in the town of Nazareth, but one day he had to go all the way to Bethlehem with Mary even though she was going to have a baby.

While they were in Bethlehem, the baby was born — it was Mary's first child, and she dressed him up in baby clothes and made a bed for him in a stable because there was no room left for them at the inn.

This is the Gospel of the Lord.

Prayers of the Faithful
God our Father, Jesus came to show your love to all people. We ask you now to help us to share this love, for all who are poor and in need, at this time.

1. We pray for people who are sleeping out this Christmas, because they have no homes to live in.
   Lord, help us to share your love.
   Lord hear us. ℞

2. We pray for people who are hungry this Christmas, because they have no food to eat.
   Lord, help us to share your love.
   Lord hear us. ℞

3. We pray for people who are cold this Christmas, because they have no warm clothes, or fuel.
   Lord, help us to share your love.
   Lord hear us. ℞

4. We pray for the sick and the old this Christmas, because they have nobody to care for them.
   Lord, help us to share your love.
   Lord hear us. ℞

5. We pray for people who are lonely and alone this Christmas, because they are forgotten by everyone.
   Lord, help us to share your love.
   Lord hear us. ℞

6. We pray for people who are sad this Christmas, because their friends have gone away or have died.
   Lord, help us to share your love.
   Lord hear us. ℞

Preparation of the Gifts
1. We bring a candle.
   Jesus, our Light, has come.
2. We bring a crown.
   Jesus, Prince of Peace, has come.
3. We bring a crucifix.
   Jesus, our Friend, has come.
4. We bring our love with the bread, the wine and the water.

Second Prayer

God our Father, we bring our gifts of bread and wine. With these gifts we bring our lives. Take our gifts in the name of Christ, your Son, who lives and reigns with you in the unity of the Holy Spirit, one God forever and ever. Amen.

Third Prayer

God our Father, we have come close to Jesus in this Communion. Help us to love one another and to make our world a happy, joyful and loving place. We make our prayer through Jesus Christ, your Son, who lives and reigns with you in the unity of the Holy Spirit, one God forever and ever. Amen.

Final Blessing

Go in peace, to love God.

13. PRAYER

Today we are thinking about prayer. Prayer is being with God, listening and talking to him. Jesus often prayed. He went to the Temple, or the mountains, or the garden to be alone with his friends and to have time to speak to his Father.

First Prayer
God our Father, you love us. We praise you and thank you for everything that we are and have. We make this prayer through Jesus, your Son, who lives and reigns with you in the unity of the Holy Spirit, one God forever and ever. Amen.

First Reading   Lk 11:46-55
This reading is Mary's prayer, the Magnificat.
Mary, the Mother of Jesus, put her trust in God.
She knew she could trust him, so she prayed.

I praise the Lord, for he is good,
he makes me glad!
I am young and I am poor,
and yet he comes and chooses me!
And from now on,
everyone will say that he has blessed me.

The Lord is strong, the Lord is generous,
stretching out his hand to help the sick,
feeding hungry people with good food,
looking after people everywhere!

Long ago he said that he would help us.
Now the Lord has kept his promise perfectly!
He has not forgotten his own people,
he has come to rescue them
and keep them safe!

This is the Word of the Lord.

Responsorial Psalm Ps 27:6-7
God is someone we can trust so we pray to him.
RESPONSE: Blessed be God!

1. Blessed be God!
   He listens to me.
   He hears me, when I pray for help. ℟

2. I trust the Lord,
   For he is strong. ℟

3. I thank the Lord,
   For he takes care of me. ℟

Second Reading Rom 8:26, 27
This reading comes from one of the letters of St Paul. The Holy Spirit will help us to pray if we don't know what to say.

Dear friends,
sometimes we find it hard to say our prayers!
But remember we have a special friend, the Holy Spirit, and he will help us.

Sometimes we don't know what to say to God, but the Holy Spirit will help us to pray without using words, and God will understand.

This is the Word of the Lord.

Gospel Acclamation
Alleluia, alleluia,
When you say your prayers don't worry so much about the things you want. Remember that you have a Father in heaven who knows all about the things you need.
Alleluia.

Gospel Reading Lk 11:1-4
This reading is from the gospel of St Luke. Jesus prays to his Father — so should we!

One day Jesus was saying his prayers and when he had finished, one of his friends said, "Teach us to pray!" So Jesus told them to say this prayer:

54

"Father,
we want everyone to praise you, and we want your kingdom to grow
better and better until it is perfect.

"Give us enough food each day,
forgive us when we do wrong,
just as we forgive others when they do wrong to us,
and help us when we are put to the test."

This is the Gospel of the Lord.

Prayers of the Faithful

God our Father, we know you care for us. We ask you now to listen
to our prayers.

1. O God, you are great.
   Help us to praise you.
   Lord hear us. ℟

2. O God, you care for us.
   Help us to trust you.
   Lord hear us. ℟

3. O God, you are good.
   Help us to love you.
   Lord hear us. ℟

4. O God, you are kind.
   Help us to be sorry when we fail to love.
   Lord hear us. ℟

5. O God, you are always giving.
   Help us to be thankful for all your gifts.
   Lord hear us. ℟

6. O God, you listen to us.
   Help us and all our friends in need.
   Lord hear us. ℟

Preparation of the Gifts

1. We bring our toys.
   We pray as we play.

55

2. We bring our books.
   We pray as we learn.
3. We bring a missalette.
   We pray in church and at home.
3. We bring our love with the bread, the wine and the water.

Second Prayer
God our Father, we bring you our gifts to thank you for what you have given us. Hear our prayers through Jesus, your Son, who lives and reigns with you in the unity of the Holy Spirit, one God forever and ever. Amen.

Third Prayer
God our Father, you have brought us close to Jesus in Holy Communion. Help us to pray often and well, like Jesus. Help us to pray in school, at play and in church. We ask this through Jesus, your Son, who lives and reigns with you in the unity of the Holy Spirit, one God forever and ever. Amen.

Final Blessing
Go in peace, to love God.

14. HELPING CHILDREN IN NEED

First Prayer

God our Father, you have given us many good gifts. Help us to be concerned for children in need, help us to do all we can and to share our good things with them. We ask this through Jesus, your Son, who lives and reigns with you in the unity of the Holy Spirit, one God forever and ever. Amen.

First Reading   Is 58:3, 4, 7, 8

This reading comes from the Book of a wise man called Isaiah. He tells us that God wants us to help the poor and the hungry so that the world can be full of his goodness and love.

God says:
Remember,
You must share things.
You must feed the hungry, and get houses for the poor people, and buy clothes for the people who haven't got enough.

If you do this,
You will make the whole world bright.
You will be like the sun that fills the sky with light each morning.

This is the Word of the Lord.

Responsorial Psalm   Ps 71:12-14, 18-19

God our Father wants us to know that he doesn't forget the poor. He will take care of those who cannot help themselves.

RESPONSE: Never forget what the Lord has done.

1. God will remember the poor when they cry.
   He will never forget them.
   He will take care of the weak.
   He will take care of the helpless. ℟

2. God is loving and he is kind.
   He will remember them.
   He will not forget them when they are in danger. ℟

3. God will not leave them to die of starvation,
   for he loves them too much. ℟

4. Blessed be God!
   He can work wonders.
   Let the whole world be full of his goodness and love! ℟

Second Reading   Rom 8:16-20

In this reading St Paul tells us that God wants us to work with him and to help each other.

The world is a place where God works for all that is worthwhile, alongside those who love him. We are fellow-workers of God. This is what he is calling us to be. The earth itself is being spoilt by the way people live. It is waiting for the time when the people who live on it will live, not as they do now, but as members of God's family, with mercy and gentleness, sharing it together.

This is the Word of the Lord.

Gospel Acclamation
Alleluia, alleluia,
"Go help everyone, everywhere, to follow me," says the Lord.
Alleluia.

Gospel Reading   Jn 21:15-17

This reading is from the gospel of St John.
It tells us that Jesus wants us to look after his friends.

After breakfast Jesus turned to Peter as they walked along, and called him by his own name, Simon:

"Simon," he said, "do you love me more than anything else?"
"Yes, sir," said Peter, "you know I love you."
"Look after my friends," said Jesus.

Jesus spoke to Peter a second time:
"Simon," he said, "do you love me?"
"Yes, sir," said Peter, "you know I love you."
"Look after my friends," said Jesus.

Then a third time, Jesus spoke to Peter:
"Simon," he said, "do you love me?"
For Jesus to ask him this question three times upset Peter.
"Sir," he said, "you know all about me. You of all people know
I love you."
"Look after my friends," said Jesus.

This is the Gospel of the Lord.

Prayers of the Faithful

God our Father, we come to you today with our own needs and the
needs of children everywhere.

1. We pray for children who are hungry.
   Give them the food and drink they need today. We pray to the
   Lord hear us. ℞ Lord.

2. We pray for children who are cold.
   Give them clothes and warmth today. We pray to the Lord
   Lord hear us. ℞

3. We pray for children who are sick.
   Give them comfort and healing today. We pray to the lord
   Lord hear us. ℞

4. We pray for children who are frightened.
   Give them love and peace today. We pray to the Lord
   Lord hear us. ℞

5. We pray for children who are lonely.
   Give them happiness and friendship today. We pray to the Lord
   Lord hear us. ℞

6. We pray for people everywhere, at home and all over the world,
   who work with children, and who lovingly care for them.
   Give them the help and strength they need. We pray to the Lord
   Lord hear us. ℞

Preparation of the Gifts

1. We bring our mission boxes.
   We do without things we like, so that we can give to others.

2. We bring a loaf of bread.
   Our savings help to feed the hungry.
3. We bring our love with the bread, the wine and the water.

Second Prayer
God our Father, we bring ourselves to you with our gifts of bread and wine. May we grow in your love by our sharing, and by helping children in need. We ask this through Jesus, your Son, who lives and reigns with you in the unity of the Holy Spirit, one God forever and ever. Amen.

Third Prayer
God our Father, may this Holy Communion help us to love each other more, and to work for the love and happiness of children everywhere. We ask this through Jesus, your Son, who lives and reigns with you in the unity of the Holy Spirit, one God forever and ever. Amen.

Final Blessing
Go in peace, to love God and to help children in need.

15. GOD'S GIFT OF WATER

Today we are thinking about God's gift of water. It gives us a lot of enjoyment, and it is very necessary too. When we think about it, we think about God's greatness.

First Prayer

God our Father, you have given us this important gift of water. May it help us to know you and your work better. We ask this through Jesus, your Son, who lives and reigns with you in the unity of the Holy Spirit, one God forever and ever. Amen.

First Reading   Ps 64:10-14

This reading is a song praising God for the gift of water which gives life to everything.

You are the one who sends down the early rain to prepare the soil for the seeds.

You are the one who gathers rain into the rivers to carry water to the crops.

You are the one who gives us gentle showers to soak into the hard-ploughed fields, to soften the earth and make the plants sprout and grow.

This is the Word of the Lord.

Responsorial Psalm

The Responsorial Psalm is about the wonders of water. We praise God for water that is so useful, and we thank him for this gift which gives us so much enjoyment and so much pleasure.

RESPONSE: Bless the Lord our God.

1. For the beauty of water, bless the Lord.
   For water that shines and reflects, bless the Lord. ℟

2. For the gushing sound of a waterfall, bless the Lord.
   For the tapping sound of the rain, bless the Lord. ℟

3. For shining lakes and flowing rivers, bless the Lord.
   For rushing brooks and roaring waves, bless the Lord. ℟

4. For cool water to quench our thirst, bless the Lord.
   For water that gives life and growth, bless the Lord. ℟

5. For water that washes and cleans, bless the Lord.
   For water that gives power, bless the Lord. ℟

6. For the waters of Baptism, bless the Lord. ℟

Second Reading   Ex 15:22-25, 27
This reading is from the Book of Moses. When Moses and the People of God were on their way to the Promised Land, they had to cross the desert and everything became hot and sandy. Then they ran out of water.

They walked for three whole days until they had used up all their water. But when they looked for some more water, they could only find a pool where the water was too horrible to drink.

Everyone grumbled at Moses, and said, "What are we going to drink now?" So Moses asked God to help him, and God did not let him down.

Moses found a special kind of wood that he could put into the water to make it nice to drink again. Then everyone could have as much water as they wanted.

Not very long afterwards, they came to a place where there were lots of palm trees and seven pools of clean drinking water, and so they pitched their tents there and set up camp.

This is the Word of the Lord.

Gospel Acclamation
Alleluia, alleluia.
Lord, you are really the Saviour of the world.
Give me the living water, so that I may never get thirsty.
Alleluia.

Gospel Reading   Jn 4:3, 6-8, 27-28
This reading is from the gospel of St John. In this story, Jesus and his friends were very thirsty, but they couldn't drink any water, because it was right down at the bottom of a deep well.

One day Jesus and his friends had to go from Judea to Galilee. They walked all through the morning until they were tired. Then they came to a place called "Jacob's Well" and stopped there for a rest.

Jesus sat down beside the well outside the town, while his friends went to buy some food, and as he sat there, a woman came along with a jug, to get some water from the well.

Jesus asked this woman for a drink.
At first the woman was surprised that Jesus spoke to her because she did not know him at all. But they soon began to talk to each other, and they were still talking when the others came back with the food. And she left her jug behind when she went away, so they could all have a drink of water from the well.

This is the Gospel of the Lord.

Prayers of the Faithful
God our Father, in our world there are so many people in need. Let us pray that they may be safe and happy.

1. We pray for people living in dry lands, who have very little water.
   Lord hear us. ℞

2. We pray for people who have too much water, and whose homes or lands have been flooded.
   Lord hear us. ℞

3. We pray for people who do not have enough to eat and drink.
   Lord hear us. ℞

4. We pray for the sick, especially for our own friends.
   May our Lady of Lourdes help them to get well.
   Lord hear us. ℞

Preparation of the Gifts
1. We bring Holy Water and the Easter Candle.
   God uses water to bring us into his family.
2. We bring a towel and a sponge.
   Water washes and cleans.
3. We bring a glass of water.
   Water gives life.
4. We bring our love with the bread, the wine and the water.

Second Prayer

God our Father, we give you these gifts of bread and wine. With them we give you our whole lives. Help us to share the Good News. We make our prayer through Jesus, your Son, who lives and reigns with you in the unity of the Holy Spirit, one God forever and ever. Amen.

Third Prayer

God our Father, you have given us Jesus in this Mass. Help us to grow in his love. We ask this through Jesus, your Son, who lives and reigns with you in the unity of the Holy Spirit, one God forever and ever. Amen.

Blessing the School with Holy Water

God our Father, bless this school. Fill the hearts of your children with goodness. Bless the footsteps of all who come to our school. May every person who comes in be the better for it.

God our Father, bless this room. Bless its four corners. Bless all of us here today.

May the blessing of God be upon us all, in the name of the Father, and of the Son, and of the Holy Spirit.

Final Blessing

Go in peace, to love God. Amen.

16. JESUS, THE LAMB OF GOD

The theme of this Mass is Jesus, the Lamb of God. A lamb is meek, gentle, innocent and strong. Jesus is meek, gentle, strong and full of goodness. We ask God in this Mass to help us to know better the gentle and strong Jesus, and to follow his ways.

First Prayer

God our Father, Jesus is the Lamb of God. Help us to be patient, gentle and strong like him. We make our prayer through Jesus, your Son, who lives and reigns with you in the unity of the Holy Spirit, one God forever and ever. Amen.

First Reading

The first reading is a poem written by Katharine Tynan.
She tells us that when she sees the sheep and lambs on the road they remind her of Jesus, the Lamb of God.

All in the April evening
April airs were abroad;
The sheep with their little lambs
Pass'd me by on the road.

The sheep with their little lambs
Pass'd me by on the road;
All in the April evening
I thought on the Lamb of God.

Up in the blue, blue mountains
Dewy pastures are sweet:
Rest for the little bodies,
Rest for the little feet.

All in the April evening,
April airs were abroad;
I saw the sheep with their lambs,
And thought on the Lamb of God.

Second Reading
Ex 12:3, 13

This reading from the Book of Moses tells us how the People of God were saved by the blood of a lamb.

Each family took a sheep or a goat and killed it. Then they used its meat for the meal. The family took some of the blood and put it on the door-posts, and above the doors of the houses where the lambs were eaten.

This was a sign that the family belonged to God.

This is the Word of the Lord.

Responsorial Psalm
Ps 3:6-7

This is a song of praise to God. We know we are safe with him.

RESPONSE: Lord, I am safe with you.

1. Lord, you look after me.
   I am safe with you. ℟

2. I go to bed at night and fall asleep and nothing worries me. ℟

3. I wake up safe and sound for you protect me. ℟

Third Reading
Rev 4:1-2, 4, 8

In this reading St John tells of a vision that he had of heaven. He tells us what he saw there.

I looked. I saw a huge crowd — no one could count all the people. They stood in front of the throne, and in front of the Lamb.

They were dressed in white robes. They were holding palms in their hands. They called out in a loud voice:

'Victory to our God who sits on the throne and to the Lamb.'

This is the Word of the Lord.

Gospel Acclamation
Alleluia, alleluia,
There is the Lamb of God,
who takes away the sins of the world.
Alleluia.

Gospel Reading   Lk 3:11-16
In this reading we hear John the Baptist calling Jesus, "the Lamb of God".

Everyone thought John was going to be the Great King, and they all began to get excited. But John said: 'I am not the Great King that God has promised to send. Someone else is coming after me, and he is much more important than I am. In fact, he is so great that I am not even good enough to untie his shoe laces!'

The next day John saw Jesus coming to him and said: 'There is the Lamb of God, who takes away the sin of the world. This is the one I was talking about when I said: "A man is coming after me, but he is much more important than I am."

This is the Gospel of the Lord.

Prayers of the Faithful
God our Father, we thank you for your goodness and love. We thank you for your care and faithfulness. We pray for the needs of others and for ourselves.

1. We pray for our parents.
   Keep them always healthy, and full of happiness.
   Lord hear us. ℞

2. We pray for our teachers.
   Keep them always loving, and full of care.
   Lord hear us. ℞

3. We pray for children.
   Keep them always gentle, and full of goodness.
   Lord hear us. ℞

4. We pray for the sick.
   Keep them always patient, and full of trust and hope.
   Lord hear us. ℞

5. We pray for our friends who have died.
   Keep them with you forever in the happiness of heaven.
   Lord hear us. ℞

Preparation of the Gifts
1. We bring a shepherd's crook.
   Jesus is the Lamb of God and our shepherd.
2. We bring a crucifix.
   Jesus takes away the sin of the world.
3. We bring our love with the bread, the wine and the water.

Second Prayer
God our Father, take these our gifts of bread and wine and take us too. May we always be ready to follow Jesus, the Lamb of God, wherever he leads us. We make our prayer through Jesus, your Son, who lives and reigns with you in the unity of the Holy Spirit, one God forever and ever. Amen.

Third Prayer
God our Father, we are close to Jesus, the Lamb of God, in this communion. May we stay close to him always and never stray far away from him. We make this prayer through Jesus Christ, your Son, who lives and reigns with you in the unity of the Holy Spirit, one God forever and ever. Amen.

Final Blessing
Go in peace, to love God.

17. FRIENDS ARE A GIFT

The theme of this Mass is friends.
A faithful friend is one of the best gifts that God has given us. We are very
lucky to have friends around us — to play with, to talk to, and to help us.
Today we think of all of our friends and we thank God for them. We thank
God too for the happiness we can have with them.

First Prayer

God our Father, we thank you for our friends. Help us to be true
friends to each other and to love one another like real friends. We
make our prayer through Jesus, your Son, who lives and reigns with
you in the unity of the Holy Spirit, one God forever and ever. Amen.

First Reading   Phil 3:8, 10

St Paul is telling us in this reading that Jesus is a great friend to have, especially
when we feel sorry for ourselves, or sad. We can be sure that Jesus will always
understand our troubles and that he will be a real friend to us.

Dear friends,
Nothing could be better than knowing Jesus!
I would give up everything, just to stay friends with him.

Remember how much he suffered and don't forget that we can always
share our troubles with him when things go wrong.

This is the Word of the Lord.

Responsorial Psalm   Ps 62:7-9

This is a song of praise to God for his love, care and friendship at all times.

RESPONSE: Lord God, I am happy to be with you.

1. At night, I lie in bed and think of you, Lord God. ℟

2. I lie there in the darkness of the night and remember how good
   you are, for you have always helped me. ℟

3. I am like a little bird that clings to its mother. ℟

4. You are like the mighty eagle who spreads its wings above its young
   to protect them. ℟

5. I am happy to lie here in the dark under the shadow of your wings,
   Lord God. ℟

Gospel Acclamation
Alleluia, alleluia.
I want you to be my friends and be happy with me.
Alleluia.

Gospel Reading Jn 15:15-17
St John is telling us in this reading that Jesus wants us to be his friends. He doesn't want us just to work for him.

One day Jesus said:
'I don't want you just to work for me and do as you're told.
'I want you to be my friends and be happy with me.

'But remember,
you did not choose me; I chose you to be my friends and I want you to be friends with each other.'

This is the Gospel of the Lord.

Prayers of the Faithful
God our Father, you are the special friend of little children. You said to your friends, 'Don't stop the children from coming to me. Bring them back.'
Put your arms around us now and bless us as we pray.

1. Bless our fathers and mothers.
   Help them to be real friends together.
   Lord hear us. ℟

2. Bless all of us, your children, as we work, play and pray together.
   Help us to be real friends together.
   Lord hear us. ℟

3. Bless the children who are lonely, forgotten, and without friends.
   Help us to be real friends together.
   Lord hear us. ℟

4. Bless the children who are unhappy because they have no friends.
   Help us to be real friends together.
   Lord hear us. ℟

5. Bless the children around the world who are cold, hungry and unhappy.
   Help us to be real friends together.
   Lord hear us. ℞

Preparation of the Gifts
1. We bring some flowers.
   We give flowers to friends.
2. We bring a globe.
   We remember our friends around the world.
3. We bring our love with the bread, the wine and the water.

Second Prayer
God our Father, we, your friends, bring to you now ourselves and all our friends. Bless us all and put your loving arms around us. We make this prayer through Jesus Christ, your Son, who lives and reigns with you in the unity of the Holy Spirit, one God forever and ever. Amen.

Communion Litany
RESPONSE: Thank you God, for friends.

1. For friends who talk to me,
   And for friends who share with me. ℞

2. For friends who play with me,
   And for friends who help me. ℞

3. For friends who comfort me,
   And for friends who cheer me up when I'm sad. ℞

4. For friends who are kind to me,
   And for friends who tell me the truth about myself. ℞

5. For friends who understand me,
   And for friends who make me happy. ℞

Third Prayer
God our Father, you have given us Jesus our friend, in this Holy Communion. Help us to be his friends forever and ever. We make this prayer through Jesus, your Son, who lives and reigns with you in the unity of the Holy Spirit, one God forever and ever. Amen.

Final Blessing
Go in peace, to love God and always be his friend.

18. GOD IS OUR ROCK

Today we are thinking about rocks and stones — big, heavy rocks and stones that are very hard to break and cannot be moved. Nothing can shake or hurt them. These make us think of God, who is our rock, always the same.

First Prayer

God our Father, you have made rocks and stones that are big and strong. May they always remind us that you are great. We make this prayer through our Lord Jesus Christ, your Son, who lives and reigns with you in the unity of the Holy Spirit, one God forever and ever. Amen.

First Reading   Acts 6:2-6, 8, 10-12
                                                            7:57, 59, 60

This reading comes from the story of the apostles. St Stephen forgives the people who used stones in a very wrong way. They used them to kill him.

One day, the twelve apostles called a meeting of the friends of Jesus, and said: we need someone to help us to give out food and look after people. Then *we* can teach and pray.

So they picked out Philip and Stephen and five others.

Then they prayed for them and they blessed them, stretching their hands over them.

Stephen did wonderful things, for he was very clever, and the Holy Spirit helped him. But some people told lies about him and had him arrested and put in prison.

The judge asked Stephen questions, but no one would listen to his answers.

They put their hands over their ears, so they couldn't hear what he was saying. Then they pulled him to a place outside the city and they threw stones at him until they killed him.

But before he died, Stephen said, "Lord Jesus, I give you my life! Do not blame them for doing wrong!"

This is the Word of the Lord.

Responsorial Psalm
The Bible tells us many times that God is like a rock or a mountain of stone. When we see a mountain or a great rock, we think of God.

RESPONSE: God is our rock.

1. A rock is solid.
   A rock is strong. ℟

2. A rock is big.
   A rock is always there. ℟

3. A rock is not afraid of the dark.
   A rock is not afraid of anything. ℟

4. A rock has caves for people to hide in.
   A rock gives a home to birds and animals. ℟

5. A rock never runs away.
   A great rock can see the country all around. ℟

Second Reading   Mt 7:21, 24-27
This reading is from the gospel of St Matthew. If we listen to Jesus, and get on with what he tells us to do we will be as safe as a house built on a rock.

"It's no good just saying that you will do what my Father wants! You must really get on with it!
"But if you do as I tell you, you will be as safe as the man who built his house on a rock.
The rains came and the land became flooded.
The wind blew and lashed against the house.
But it did not fall down, because it was built firmly on a rock."

This is the Word of the Lord.

Gospel Acclamation
Alleluia, alleluia.
God is my rock.
I find my strength in him.
Alleluia.

74

Gospel Reading   Mt 16: 13-18
This reading is from the gospel of St Matthew.
Jesus picked Peter to be a kind of foundation stone — a strong rocky base for his Church. Peter's job was to build a strong family of God, so he needed to be as strong as a rock.

One day when Jesus was praying with his disciples, he asked them, "Who do the people say I am?"
They answered him that some people said he was John the Baptist, others Elijah, others Jeremiah or one of the prophets.
"But you", he said, "who do you say I am?"
And Simon Peter replied,
"You are Christ, the Son of God."
"You are a lucky man, Simon," said Jesus, "for my Father in heaven has revealed this to you. Now I tell you that you are Peter (which means rock), and on this rock I will build my church."

This is the Gospel of the Lord.

Prayers of the Faithful
God our Father, you are like a rock, you are strong and you do not change.
Listen to us as we pray.

1. Help us to be strong, kind and loving.
   Lord hear us. ℟

2. Help us to be strong and to forgive those who hurt us.
   Lord hear us. ℟

3. Help us to be strong and to share with our friends.
   Lord hear us. ℟

4. Help us to be strong and to do what we are told.
   Lord hear us. ℟

5. Help us to be strong and to help whenever we can.
   Lord hear us. ℟

Preparation of the Gifts
1. We bring pebbles from the beach.
2. We bring a piece of coal.
3. We bring a diamond ring.
4. We bring our love with the bread, the wine and the water.

Second Prayer
God our Father, we give you ourselves with these gifts of bread and wine. Help us to be strong, to do good. We ask this through Jesus, your Son, who lives and reigns with you in the unity of the Holy Spirit, one God forever and ever. Amen.

Communion Litany
RESPONSE: Thank you God our Father.

1. For stone for walls,
   For stone for homes. ℞

2. For stone for crosses,
   For stone for churches. ℞

3. For stone for altars,
   For stone for monuments. ℞

4. For stone for monasteries,
   For stone for statues. ℞

5. For stone for castles,
   For stone for bridges. ℞

6. For stones and rocks everywhere —
   they make us think of you. ℞

Third Prayer
God our Father, you have given us Jesus and you are with us all the time, strong and sure as a rock. Help us to live as your loving children. We ask this through Jesus, your Son, who lives and reigns with you in the unity of the Holy Spirit, one God forever and ever. Amen.

Final Blessing
Go in peace, to love God.

19. THE SKY

The theme today is the sky — the sun, the moon, the stars and the planets that God has made. When we see the sky we thank God, so great and powerful, so gentle and loving.

First Prayer
God our Father, you are Creator of the whole world. You made the great sky by your power. Help us to know your greatness and your power. We make our prayer through Jesus, your Son, who lives and reigns with you in the unity of the Holy Spirit, one God forever and ever. Amen.

First Reading   Gen 1:9-10, 14-18
This reading tells us that God is the Creator of the sun, the moon, the stars and the sky. And God made them all very good.

God said:
'Let there be dry land!
(and he called it "the Earth").

Let there be water round the land!
(and he called it "the Sea").

Let there be a roof over the land!
(and he called it "the Sky").'

And God said it was good.

God said:
'Let there be a light to shine during the day!
(and he called it "the Sun").

Let there be smaller lights to shine at night!
(and he called them "the Moon" and "the Stars").'

And God said it was good.

This is the Word of the Lord.

Responsorial Psalm   Ps 139:1-9

*God our Father gives us so much. We praise and thank him. We praise
and thank him especially for the sky, the sun, the moon and the stars.*

RESPONSE: We praise and thank you Father.
          You are good to us.

1. You made the sky,
   For you are wise.
   You made the earth,
   For you are kind. ℟

2. You gave the sun,
   To shine in the day.
   You gave the moon,
   To shine in the night. ℟

3. You made the stars,
   To light the sky at night.
   You made the clouds,
   To colour the sky by day. ℟

Second Reading   Ps 18:1-5

*God 'speaks' to us and he doesn't have to use words. The best way to find
out what God is saying to us, is to look around and see the beauty of his
world, and especially the beauty of the sky.*

Silently,
Each morning,
without a word,
without the slightest sound,
the golden sun appears,
and rises,
high up in the sky,
giving heat and light to everyone.
How beautiful!
How marvellous!
Each day, the sky tells all of us,
that God is wonderful.

Silently,
each morning,
without a word,
without the slightest sound,
the sky gives each of us this message
across the whole wide world
as each new day begins.
How beautiful!
How marvellous!
Each day, the sky tells all of us,
that God is wonderful.

This is the Word of the Lord.

Gospel Acclamation
Alleluia, alleluia,
Glory be to God on high,
And peace, to all who are his friends.
Alleluia.

Gospel Reading   Lk 2:8-14
In this reading we see how God used the light in the sky to bring the Good News of the Birth of Jesus.

Out on the hillside near Bethlehem, some shepherds were looking after their sheep that night. Everything was still and quiet, under the stars. The shepherds were lying on the grass, half-asleep. Suddenly, an angel appeared to them. The shepherds were afraid. They had never seen an angel before.

The angel said to them:
'Don't be afraid, shepherds. I have some good news for you. The Lord is born tonight, in a stable in Bethlehem. Go and see him. You will find him lying, wrapped up, in a manger.'

All at once, the whole sky was filled with the music of heaven, and the angel sang in a clear voice:
'Glory to God on high,
And peace to all who are is friends.'

This is the Gospel of the Lord.

Prayers of the Faithful

God our Father, we bring to you in prayer the needs of the people who work for us by the bright light of the day and in the dark of the night.

1. We pray for our parents who work and care for us night and day.
   Bless their work.
   Lord hear us. ℞

2. We pray for the people who work for us on the streets, in the towns and out on the sea.
   Bless their work.
   Lord hear us. ℞

3. We pray for the people who work for us on the farms, up in the sky, and deep down underground.
   Bless their work.
   Lord hear us. ℞

4. We pray for the people who work for us in the schools, in the hospitals, and in factories.
   Bless their work.
   Lord hear us. ℞

5. We pray for ourselves. Help us to see your love and goodness in the people who work for us, and in the beauty of the sky above us. Lord hear us. ℞

Second Prayer

God our Father, we bring our gifts to you now. With them, we bring all the good things of the world, especially the sky, the planets and the stars. Help us always to know you in the beauty of your world. We make our prayer through Jesus Christ, your Son, who lives and reigns with you in the unity of the Holy Spirit, one God forever and ever. Amen.

Communion   Recorded Music: *'The Planets' Op. 32: Holst*

Third Prayer

God our Father, we have come close to Jesus at this holy meal. Help us to bring his power and love to everyone we meet today and everyday. We make our prayer through Jesus Christ, your Son, who lives and reigns with you in the unity of the Holy Spirit, one God forever and ever. Amen.

Final Blessing

Go in peace, and thank God for all his great gifts. Amen.

Go in peace, and thank God for the beauty of the sky. Amen.

Go in peace, and thank God for the beauty and goodness of people. Amen.

20. GOD TAKES CARE OF FLOWERS

God must like flowers because he has filled our world with beautiful flowers of every colour shape and size, and he takes good care of them all the time. If God takes such care of the flowers that soon die, he must surely take very good care of all of us too.

First Prayer
God our Father, you have made this world beautiful with flowers of every colour, and you take good care of them. Help us to know how much you care for us, too. We make this prayer through Jesus Christ, your Son, who lives and reigns with you in the unity of the Holy Spirit, one God forever and ever. Amen.

First Reading   Is 27:3, 4, 6
God likes flowers and he takes good care of them. He knows that they make the world beautiful, and that we like them too.

God says:

I am a gardener, and I look after my garden all day and all night.

I keep watering all my plants because I don't want them to dry up or their leaves will fall off.

If I find any weeds I will pull them up.

Then the whole of my garden will be filled with flowers.

This is the Word of the Lord.

Responsorial Psalm   Ps 1:3
We praise God the Father who gives us beautiful trees and flowers and takes care of them in summer and in winter.

RESPONSE: Give praise to God.

1. Down by the river is a good place for trees.
   If the water flows near them, they will not grow dry. ℟

2. Their leaves are not withered, they stay green and alive.
   And each year their branches are covered with fruit. ℟

3. The child that is good is like a tree by the river.
   God will look after him. ℟

4. God will protect him,
   and like a tree by the river he will grow strong. ℟

Second Reading   Song 2:11-13
Each year it is the same. Most flowers stop growing in winter but rise up again in spring to beautify the world.

When winter is finished, and the rain has stopped falling, then the plants begin to grow.

The birds sing and leaves appear on the trees and at last you can smell the perfume of the flowers.

This is the time to sing for joy!

This is the Word of the Lord.

Gospel Acclamation
Alleluia, alleluia.
If God takes so much trouble over the flowers
then he will certainly take good care of you.
Alleluia.

Gospel Reading   Lk 12:27-28
Jesus knew that God took good care of the flowers. He wanted people to know that God takes care of everything else as well, and especially of all of us.

One day Jesus said:
Look at the flowers!

They don't worry about anything, and yet they look more beautiful than a King dressed in his best clothes!

So don't worry about yourselves. If God takes so much care of the flowers then he will certainly take good care of you.

This is the Gospel of the Lord.

Prayers of the Faithful

God our Father, you watch over us and care for us. You care for us in dark days and in bright days. You care for us in winter and in summer. We thank you for your care of us all, and now we pray for our needs.

1. Bless our bishop and our priests who care for us in a special way.
   Lord hear us. ℟

2. Bless our parents whom you have given us to care for us.
   Lord hear us. ℟

3. Bless ourselves so that we will always make things easy for those who care for us.
   Lord hear us. ℟

4. Bless children everywhere and the people who care for them.
   Lord hear us. ℟

5. Bless the sick and those who care for them.
   Lord hear us. ℟

6. Bless the people who feel nobody cares about them.
   Lord hear us. ℟

Preparation of the Gifts

1. We bring flowers.
   Flowers are God's gift to us.
2. We bring water.
   God cares for the flowers and he cares for us too.
3. We bring our love with the bread, the wine and the water.

Second Prayer

God our Father, we bring you ourselves and our gift of flowers. May flowers ever bring us nearer to you. We make this prayer through Jesus Christ, your Son, who lives and reigns with you in the unity of the Holy Spirit, one God forever and ever. Amen.

Communion Litany
RESPONSE: We thank you God.

1. For flowers that are red, blue, orange and yellow,
   and for flowers that are white, golden, purple and lilac. ℞

2. For flowers that sway in the breeze,
   and for flowers that open in the sunlight. ℞

3. For flowers that smell sweetly,
   and for flowers that make us joyful and happy. ℞

4. For flowers that grow straight and tall,
   and for flowers that send out roots for food. ℞

5. For flowers that are full of life and growing,
   and for flowers that speak to us of God. ℞

Third Prayer
God our Father, we have come close to your Son, Jesus, in this Holy Communion. May the flowers, that speak to us of your goodness, ever help us to stay close to you. We make our prayer through Jesus Christ, your Son, who lives and reigns with you in the unity of the Holy Spirit, one God forever and ever. Amen.

Final Blessing
Go in peace, to love God.

Faith and Little Children:
A Guide for Parents and teachers
Karen Leslie
Faith and Little Children is a most needed volume on the subject of introducing 3–6 year olds to the Catholic religion. Catechists and parents of pre-school/kindergarten age children will appreciate the concrete instructions on how to facilitate children's understanding of our catholic community. The activities are aimed at approaching youngsters through the senses and through actual experience.

ISBN: 0-89622404-X

Fr. Ike's Stories for Children
Fr. Isaias Powers
This delightful and heart-warming book grew out of the author's parish missions and retreats, where he first began telling these stories. The book contains 12 animal stories, each with a moral. The children are entertained, then led to see the Christian values that are the core of the message.

ISBN: 0-89622370-1

Celebrations of the Word for Children
Pastors, worship committees, church educators—all who rejoice in sharing the Word of God with young people will find these Scripture services contain two liturgies for each school-year month, plus extras for Christmas and Lent.

Cycle A, ISBN: 0-89622-308-6
Cycle B, ISBN: 0-89622-332-9
Cycle C, ISBN: 0-89622-362-0

Summertime, Bibletime
William J. DeAngelis
Vacation Bible School guidebook for church leaders set up to give years of use for one- or two-week programs. Highlights: suggested arts and crafts, games, Bible plays, staff organization, publicity, etc. Ideal for elementary grades.

ISBN: 0-89622-322-1

Eucharist:
Our Communal Celebration
Marie McIntyre
Parents and teachers of First Communion classes gain insight into the relationship of communion and eucharist to an understanding of church and community.

ISBN: 0-89622-077-X

Prayer Services with Young People
Donal Neary, SJ
Here's a collection of prayer and liturgical services for use with young people from 14 years old and up. There are both eucharistic and non-eucharistic services and liturgies, which are suitable for use in different settings.

ISBN: 0-948183-09-8

Lectionary for Masses with Children
Helping young people discover and understand the Good News is what these books are all about. Created by a team of educational, biblical, and liturgical experts, these lectionaries are simple, reverent, and very effective. Texts for the readings are taken from the *Jerusalem Bible,* making them most appropriate for liturgical use.

Year A, ISBN: 0-89622-411-1
Year B, ISBN: 0-89622-435-X
Year C, ISBN: 0-89622-385-X

A Bible Way of the Cross for Children
Gwen Costello
Upper primary and intermediate grade children will respond positively to *A Bible Way of the cross for Children*. Each Station starts with an appropriate Scripture passage, then moves to meditation and prayer reinforced by suggested movements, thought-provoking questions and exercises. The text is complemented by silhouette art.

ISBN: 0-89622-353-1

Praying and Doing the Stations of the Cross with Children
Diane Abajian
Kindergarten and primary grade children will be drawn to the tender, living Jesus portrayed in this prayer and activity booklet.

ISBN: 0-89622-118-0

For additional information on any of these titles:

In United Kingdom:
Columba Book Service
93 The Rise, Mount Merrion
Blackrock County, Dublin, Ireland
In U.S.A.:
Twenty-Third Publications
P.O. Box 180
185 Willow Street
Mystic, CT 06355
Toll free: 1-800-321-0411
1-203-536-2611